Fulfillment Journal

Preface

A guide to effectively using your Fulfillment Journal

Welcome to The Fulfillment Journal, begin by finding a quiet place that you can be comfortable with no distractions, then take 50 minutes, 10 mins for each area, to write down all of the things which bring you fulfillment in the 5 main areas of life.

Faith

Family

Fitness

Finance

Fun

As you begin this process consider these three questions to determine if it is true fulfillment.

1. What brings me to tears of joy?
2. What stimulates uncontrollable laughter?
3. What causes me to shout in excitement?

Once you have identified how you experience the most fulfillment in each area of your life. Now take the time to schedule one experience in for each day of the month.

Share Your Success

I invite you share your experiences of fulfillment on social media. Let me know how I can help you receive more fulfillment in your life and increase your income while you're living in your purpose and passion.

Podcast
The Fuel Your Legacy Show

Instagram
@sam.knickerbocker
@thefuelyourlegacyshow

Facebook
@Samuel Knickerbocker

YouTube
Samuel Knickerbocker

Website
https://samknickerbocker.com

Also check out Samuel's other book

"Fuel Your Legacy: 9 Pillars to Build a Meaningful Legacy"

How I Am Fulfilled in my Faith

_____

_____

_____

_____

_____

_____

_____

_____

_____

_____

_____

_____

_____

_____

_____

_____

_____

_____

_____

_____

_____

_____

_____

_____

How I Am Fulfilled in my Family

_____

_____

_____

_____

_____

_____

_____

_____

_____

_____

_____

_____

_____

_____

_____

_____

_____

_____

_____

_____

_____

_____

How I Am Fulfilled in my Fitness

How I Am Fulfilled in my Finance

_____

_____

_____

_____

_____

_____

_____

_____

_____

_____

_____

_____

_____

_____

_____

_____

_____

_____

_____

_____

_____

_____

_____

How I Am Fulfilled in Fun

Notes

Morning

Date: _____

The three things I am most grateful for today are:

1. _____
2. _____
3. _____

My top three priorities today are.

1. _____
2. _____
3. _____

Today I will experience fulfillment through:

_____

_____

_____

_____

_____

Today I will serve others by:

_____

_____

_____

_____

_____

Evening

Date: _____

How did I experience fulfillment today?

_____

_____

_____

_____

_____

_____

_____

_____

_____

What could I do in the future to experience more fulfillment?

_____

_____

_____

_____

_____

_____

_____

_____

_____

Morning

Date: _____

The three things I am most grateful for today are:

1. _____
2. _____
3. _____

My top three priorities today are.

1. _____
2. _____
3. _____

Today I will experience fulfillment through:

_____

_____

_____

_____

_____

Today I will serve others by:

_____

_____

_____

_____

_____

Evening

Date: _____

How did I experience fulfillment today?

_____

_____

_____

_____

_____

_____

_____

_____

_____

What could I do in the future to experience more fulfillment?

_____

_____

_____

_____

_____

_____

_____

_____

_____

Morning

Date: _____

The three things I am most grateful for today are:

1. _____

2. _____

3. _____

My top three priorities today are.

1. _____

2. _____

3. _____

Today I will experience fulfillment through:

_____

_____

_____

_____

_____

Today I will serve others by:

_____

_____

_____

_____

_____

Evening

Date: _____

How did I experience fulfillment today?

_____

_____

_____

_____

_____

_____

_____

_____

_____

What could I do in the future to experience more fulfillment?

_____

_____

_____

_____

_____

_____

_____

_____

_____

Morning

Date: _____

The three things I am most grateful for today are:

1. _____
2. _____
3. _____

My top three priorities today are.

1. _____
2. _____
3. _____

Today I will experience fulfillment through:

_____

_____

_____

_____

_____

Today I will serve others by:

_____

_____

_____

_____

_____

Evening

Date: _____

How did I experience fulfillment today?

_____

_____

_____

_____

_____

_____

_____

_____

_____

What could I do in the future to experience more fulfillment?

_____

_____

_____

_____

_____

_____

_____

_____

_____

Date: _____

The three things I am most grateful for today are:

1. _____
2. _____
3. _____

My top three priorities today are.

1. _____
2. _____
3. _____

Today I will experience fulfillment through:

_____

_____

_____

_____

_____

Today I will serve others by:

_____

_____

_____

_____

_____

Evening

Date: _____

How did I experience fulfillment today?

_____

_____

_____

_____

_____

_____

_____

_____

_____

What could I do in the future to experience more fulfillment?

_____

_____

_____

_____

_____

_____

_____

_____

_____

Morning

Date: _____

The three things I am most grateful for today are:

1. _____
2. _____
3. _____

My top three priorities today are.

1. _____
2. _____
3. _____

Today I will experience fulfillment through:

_____

_____

_____

_____

_____

Today I will serve others by:

_____

_____

_____

_____

_____

Evening

Date: _____

How did I experience fulfillment today?

_____

_____

_____

_____

_____

_____

_____

_____

_____

What could I do in the future to experience more fulfillment?

_____

_____

_____

_____

_____

_____

_____

_____

_____

Morning

Date: _____

The three things I am most grateful for today are:

1. _____
2. _____
3. _____

My top three priorities today are.

1. _____
2. _____
3. _____

Today I will experience fulfillment through:

_____

_____

_____

_____

_____

Today I will serve others by:

_____

_____

_____

_____

_____

Evening

Date: _____

How did I experience fulfillment today?

_____

_____

_____

_____

_____

_____

_____

_____

_____

What could I do in the future to experience more fulfillment?

_____

_____

_____

_____

_____

_____

_____

_____

_____

Morning

Date: _____

The three things I am most grateful for today are:

1. _____
2. _____
3. _____

My top three priorities today are.

1. _____
2. _____
3. _____

Today I will experience fulfillment through:

_____

_____

_____

_____

_____

Today I will serve others by:

_____

_____

_____

_____

_____

Evening

Date: _____

How did I experience fulfillment today?

_____

_____

_____

_____

_____

_____

_____

_____

_____

What could I do in the future to experience more fulfillment?

_____

_____

_____

_____

_____

_____

_____

_____

_____

Morning

Date: _____

The three things I am most grateful for today are:

1. _____

2. _____

3. _____

My top three priorities today are.

1. _____

2. _____

3. _____

Today I will experience fulfillment through:

_____

_____

_____

_____

_____

Today I will serve others by:

_____

_____

_____

_____

_____

Evening

Date: _____

How did I experience fulfillment today?

_____

_____

_____

_____

_____

_____

_____

_____

_____

What could I do in the future to experience more fulfillment?

_____

_____

_____

_____

_____

_____

_____

_____

_____

Morning

Date: _____

The three things I am most grateful for today are:

1. _____

2. _____

3. _____

My top three priorities today are.

1. _____

2. _____

3. _____

Today I will experience fulfillment through:

_____

_____

_____

_____

_____

Today I will serve others by:

_____

_____

_____

_____

_____

Evening

Date: _____

How did I experience fulfillment today?

_____

_____

_____

_____

_____

_____

_____

_____

What could I do in the future to experience more fulfillment?

_____

_____

_____

_____

_____

_____

_____

_____

Morning

Date: _____

The three things I am most grateful for today are:

1.
_____
2.
_____
3.
_____

My top three priorities today are.

1.
_____
2.
_____
3.
_____

Today I will experience fulfillment through:

_____

_____

_____

_____

_____

Today I will serve others by:

_____

_____

_____

_____

_____

Evening

Date: _____

How did I experience fulfillment today?

_____

_____

_____

_____

_____

_____

_____

_____

_____

What could I do in the future to experience more fulfillment?

_____

_____

_____

_____

_____

_____

_____

_____

_____

Morning

Date: _____

The three things I am most grateful for today are:

1. _____
2. _____
3. _____

My top three priorities today are.

1. _____
2. _____
3. _____

Today I will experience fulfillment through:

_____

_____

_____

_____

_____

Today I will serve others by:

_____

_____

_____

_____

_____

Evening

Date: _____

How did I experience fulfillment today?

_____

_____

_____

_____

_____

_____

_____

_____

_____

What could I do in the future to experience more fulfillment?

_____

_____

_____

_____

_____

_____

_____

_____

_____

Morning

Date: _____

The three things I am most grateful for today are:

1. _____
2. _____
3. _____

My top three priorities today are.

1. _____
2. _____
3. _____

Today I will experience fulfillment through:

_____

_____

_____

_____

_____

Today I will serve others by:

_____

_____

_____

_____

_____

Evening

Date: _____

How did I experience fulfillment today?

_____

_____

_____

_____

_____

_____

_____

_____

_____

What could I do in the future to experience more fulfillment?

_____

_____

_____

_____

_____

_____

_____

_____

_____

_____

Morning

Date: _____

The three things I am most grateful for today are:

1. _____

2. _____

3. _____

My top three priorities today are.

1. _____

2. _____

3. _____

Today I will experience fulfillment through:

_____

_____

_____

_____

_____

Today I will serve others by:

_____

_____

_____

_____

_____

Evening

Date: _____

How did I experience fulfillment today?

_____

_____

_____

_____

_____

_____

_____

_____

_____

What could I do in the future to experience more fulfillment?

_____

_____

_____

_____

_____

_____

_____

_____

_____

Morning

Date: _____

The three things I am most grateful for today are:

1. _____
2. _____
3. _____

My top three priorities today are.

1. _____
2. _____
3. _____

Today I will experience fulfillment through:

_____

_____

_____

_____

Today I will serve others by:

_____

_____

_____

_____

Evening

Date: _____

How did I experience fulfillment today?

_____

_____

_____

_____

_____

_____

_____

_____

_____

What could I do in the future to experience more fulfillment?

_____

_____

_____

_____

_____

_____

_____

_____

_____

Morning

Date: _____

The three things I am most grateful for today are:

1. _____

2. _____

3. _____

My top three priorities today are.

1. _____

2. _____

3. _____

Today I will experience fulfillment through:

_____

_____

_____

_____

_____

Today I will serve others by:

_____

_____

_____

_____

_____

Evening

Date: _____

How did I experience fulfillment today?

_____

_____

_____

_____

_____

_____

_____

_____

What could I do in the future to experience more fulfillment?

_____

_____

_____

_____

_____

_____

_____

_____

Morning

Date: _____

The three things I am most grateful for today are:

1. _____
2. _____
3. _____

My top three priorities today are.

1. _____
2. _____
3. _____

Today I will experience fulfillment through:

_____

_____

_____

_____

_____

Today I will serve others by:

_____

_____

_____

_____

_____

Evening

Date: _____

How did I experience fulfillment today?

_____

_____

_____

_____

_____

_____

_____

_____

_____

What could I do in the future to experience more fulfillment?

_____

_____

_____

_____

_____

_____

_____

_____

_____

Morning

Date: _____

The three things I am most grateful for today are:

1.
_____
2.
_____
3.
_____

My top three priorities today are.

1.
_____
2.
_____
3.
_____

Today I will experience fulfillment through:

_____

_____

_____

_____

_____

Today I will serve others by:

_____

_____

_____

_____

_____

Evening

Date: _____

How did I experience fulfillment today?

_____

_____

_____

_____

_____

_____

_____

_____

_____

What could I do in the future to experience more fulfillment?

_____

_____

_____

_____

_____

_____

_____

_____

_____

Morning

Date: _____

The three things I am most grateful for today are:

1. _____
2. _____
3. _____

My top three priorities today are.

1. _____
2. _____
3. _____

Today I will experience fulfillment through:

_____

_____

_____

_____

_____

Today I will serve others by:

_____

_____

_____

_____

_____

Evening

Date: _____

How did I experience fulfillment today?

_____

_____

_____

_____

_____

_____

_____

_____

_____

What could I do in the future to experience more fulfillment?

_____

_____

_____

_____

_____

_____

_____

_____

_____

Morning

Date: _____

The three things I am most grateful for today are:

1.
2.
3.

My top three priorities today are.

1.
2.
3.

Today I will experience fulfillment through:

Today I will serve others by:

Evening

Date: _____

How did I experience fulfillment today?

_____

_____

_____

_____

_____

_____

_____

_____

_____

What could I do in the future to experience more fulfillment?

_____

_____

_____

_____

_____

_____

_____

_____

_____

Morning

Date: _____

The three things I am most grateful for today are:

1. _____
2. _____
3. _____

My top three priorities today are.

1. _____
2. _____
3. _____

Today I will experience fulfillment through:

_____

_____

_____

_____

_____

Today I will serve others by:

_____

_____

_____

_____

_____

Evening

Date: _____

How did I experience fulfillment today?

_____

_____

_____

_____

_____

_____

_____

_____

_____

What could I do in the future to experience more fulfillment?

_____

_____

_____

_____

_____

_____

_____

_____

_____

Morning

Date: _____

The three things I am most grateful for today are:

1. _____

2. _____

3. _____

My top three priorities today are.

1. _____

2. _____

3. _____

Today I will experience fulfillment through:

_____

_____

_____

_____

_____

Today I will serve others by:

_____

_____

_____

_____

_____

Evening

Date: _____

How did I experience fulfillment today?

_____

_____

_____

_____

_____

_____

_____

_____

_____

What could I do in the future to experience more fulfillment?

_____

_____

_____

_____

_____

_____

_____

_____

_____

Morning

Date: _____

The three things I am most grateful for today are:

1. _____

2. _____

3. _____

My top three priorities today are.

1. _____

2. _____

3. _____

Today I will experience fulfillment through:

_____

_____

_____

_____

_____

Today I will serve others by:

_____

_____

_____

_____

_____

Evening

Date: _____

How did I experience fulfillment today?

_____

_____

_____

_____

_____

_____

_____

_____

_____

What could I do in the future to experience more fulfillment?

_____

_____

_____

_____

_____

_____

_____

_____

_____

Morning

Date: _____

The three things I am most grateful for today are:

1.
_____
2.
_____
3.
_____

My top three priorities today are.

1.
_____
2.
_____
3.
_____

Today I will experience fulfillment through:

_____

_____

_____

_____

_____

Today I will serve others by:

_____

_____

_____

_____

_____

Evening

Date: _____

How did I experience fulfillment today?

_____

_____

_____

_____

_____

_____

_____

_____

_____

What could I do in the future to experience more fulfillment?

_____

_____

_____

_____

_____

_____

_____

_____

_____

Morning

Date: _____

The three things I am most grateful for today are:

1. _____
2. _____
3. _____

My top three priorities today are.

1. _____
2. _____
3. _____

Today I will experience fulfillment through:

_____

_____

_____

_____

_____

Today I will serve others by:

_____

_____

_____

_____

_____

Evening

Date: _____

How did I experience fulfillment today?

_____

_____

_____

_____

_____

_____

_____

_____

_____

What could I do in the future to experience more fulfillment?

_____

_____

_____

_____

_____

_____

_____

_____

_____

Morning

Date: _____

The three things I am most grateful for today are:

1. _____
2. _____
3. _____

My top three priorities today are.

1. _____
2. _____
3. _____

Today I will experience fulfillment through:

_____

_____

_____

_____

_____

Today I will serve others by:

_____

_____

_____

_____

_____

Evening

Date: _____

How did I experience fulfillment today?

_____

_____

_____

_____

_____

_____

_____

_____

What could I do in the future to experience more fulfillment?

_____

_____

_____

_____

_____

_____

_____

_____

Morning

Date: _____

The three things I am most grateful for today are:

1.
_____
2.
_____
3.
_____

My top three priorities today are.

1.
_____
2.
_____
3.
_____

Today I will experience fulfillment through:

_____

_____

_____

_____

_____

Today I will serve others by:

_____

_____

_____

_____

_____

Evening

Date: _____

How did I experience fulfillment today?

_____

_____

_____

_____

_____

_____

_____

_____

_____

What could I do in the future to experience more fulfillment?

_____

_____

_____

_____

_____

_____

_____

_____

_____

Morning

Date: _____

The three things I am most grateful for today are:

1. _____

2. _____

3. _____

My top three priorities today are.

1. _____

2. _____

3. _____

Today I will experience fulfillment through:

_____

_____

_____

_____

_____

Today I will serve others by:

_____

_____

_____

_____

_____

Evening

Date: _____

How did I experience fulfillment today?

_____

_____

_____

_____

_____

_____

_____

_____

_____

What could I do in the future to experience more fulfillment?

_____

_____

_____

_____

_____

_____

_____

_____

_____

Morning

Date: _____

The three things I am most grateful for today are:

1. _____
2. _____
3. _____

My top three priorities today are.

1. _____
2. _____
3. _____

Today I will experience fulfillment through:

_____

_____

_____

_____

_____

Today I will serve others by:

_____

_____

_____

_____

_____

Evening

Date: _____

How did I experience fulfillment today?

_____

_____

_____

_____

_____

_____

_____

_____

_____

What could I do in the future to experience more fulfillment?

_____

_____

_____

_____

_____

_____

_____

_____

_____

Morning

Date: _____

The three things I am most grateful for today are:

1. _____

2. _____

3. _____

My top three priorities today are.

1. _____

2. _____

3. _____

Today I will experience fulfillment through:

_____

_____

_____

_____

_____

Today I will serve others by:

_____

_____

_____

_____

_____

Evening

Date: _____

How did I experience fulfillment today?

_____

_____

_____

_____

_____

_____

_____

_____

_____

What could I do in the future to experience more fulfillment?

_____

_____

_____

_____

_____

_____

_____

_____

_____

Morning

Date: _____

The three things I am most grateful for today are:

1. _____

2. _____

3. _____

My top three priorities today are.

1. _____

2. _____

3. _____

Today I will experience fulfillment through:

_____

_____

_____

_____

_____

Today I will serve others by:

_____

_____

_____

_____

_____

Evening

Date: _____

How did I experience fulfillment today?

_____

_____

_____

_____

_____

_____

_____

_____

What could I do in the future to experience more fulfillment?

_____

_____

_____

_____

_____

_____

_____

_____

_____

How I Am Fulfilled in my Faith

_____

_____

_____

_____

_____

_____

_____

_____

_____

_____

_____

_____

_____

_____

_____

_____

_____

_____

_____

_____

_____

How I Am Fulfilled in my Family

_____

_____

_____

_____

_____

_____

_____

_____

_____

_____

_____

_____

_____

_____

_____

_____

_____

_____

_____

_____

_____

_____

_____

_____

How I Am Fulfilled in my Fitness

How I Am Fulfilled in my Finance

_____

_____

_____

_____

_____

_____

_____

_____

_____

_____

_____

_____

_____

_____

_____

_____

_____

_____

_____

_____

How I Am Fulfilled in Fun

Notes

Morning

Date: _____

The three things I am most grateful for today are:

1.
_____
2.
_____
3.
_____

My top three priorities today are.

1.
_____
2.
_____
3.
_____

Today I will experience fulfillment through:

_____

_____

_____

_____

_____

Today I will serve others by:

_____

_____

_____

_____

_____

Evening

Date: _____

How did I experience fulfillment today?

_____

_____

_____

_____

_____

_____

_____

_____

_____

What could I do in the future to experience more fulfillment?

_____

_____

_____

_____

_____

_____

_____

_____

_____

Morning

Date: _____

The three things I am most grateful for today are:

1.
_____
2.
_____
3.
_____

My top three priorities today are.

1.
_____
2.
_____
3.
_____

Today I will experience fulfillment through:

_____

_____

_____

_____

_____

Today I will serve others by:

_____

_____

_____

_____

_____

Evening

Date: _____

How did I experience fulfillment today?

_____

_____

_____

_____

_____

_____

_____

_____

_____

What could I do in the future to experience more fulfillment?

_____

_____

_____

_____

_____

_____

_____

_____

_____

Morning

Date: _____

The three things I am most grateful for today are:

1. _____
2. _____
3. _____

My top three priorities today are.

1. _____
2. _____
3. _____

Today I will experience fulfillment through:

_____

_____

_____

_____

_____

Today I will serve others by:

_____

_____

_____

_____

_____

Evening

Date: _____

How did I experience fulfillment today?

_____

_____

_____

_____

_____

_____

_____

_____

_____

What could I do in the future to experience more fulfillment?

_____

_____

_____

_____

_____

_____

_____

_____

_____

Morning

Date: _____

The three things I am most grateful for today are:

1. _____
2. _____
3. _____

My top three priorities today are.

1. _____
2. _____
3. _____

Today I will experience fulfillment through:

_____

_____

_____

_____

_____

Today I will serve others by:

_____

_____

_____

_____

_____

Evening

Date: _____

How did I experience fulfillment today?

_____

_____

_____

_____

_____

_____

_____

_____

_____

_____

What could I do in the future to experience more fulfillment?

_____

_____

_____

_____

_____

_____

_____

_____

_____

Morning

Date: _____

The three things I am most grateful for today are:

1. _____
2. _____
3. _____

My top three priorities today are.

1. _____
2. _____
3. _____

Today I will experience fulfillment through:

_____
_____
_____
_____
_____

Today I will serve others by:

_____
_____
_____
_____
_____

Evening

Date: _____

How did I experience fulfillment today?

_____

_____

_____

_____

_____

_____

_____

_____

_____

What could I do in the future to experience more fulfillment?

_____

_____

_____

_____

_____

_____

_____

_____

_____

Morning

Date: _____

The three things I am most grateful for today are:

1.
_____
2.
_____
3.
_____

My top three priorities today are.

1.
_____
2.
_____
3.
_____

Today I will experience fulfillment through:

_____

_____

_____

_____

_____

Today I will serve others by:

_____

_____

_____

_____

_____

Evening

Date: _____

How did I experience fulfillment today?

_____

_____

_____

_____

_____

_____

_____

_____

_____

What could I do in the future to experience more fulfillment?

_____

_____

_____

_____

_____

_____

_____

_____

_____

Morning

Date: _____

The three things I am most grateful for today are:

1. _____
2. _____
3. _____

My top three priorities today are.

1. _____
2. _____
3. _____

Today I will experience fulfillment through:

_____

_____

_____

_____

_____

Today I will serve others by:

_____

_____

_____

_____

_____

Evening

Date: _____

How did I experience fulfillment today?

_____

_____

_____

_____

_____

_____

_____

_____

_____

What could I do in the future to experience more fulfillment?

_____

_____

_____

_____

_____

_____

_____

_____

_____

Morning

Date: _____

The three things I am most grateful for today are:

1. _____
2. _____
3. _____

My top three priorities today are.

1. _____
2. _____
3. _____

Today I will experience fulfillment through:

_____

_____

_____

_____

_____

Today I will serve others by:

_____

_____

_____

_____

_____

Evening

Date: _____

How did I experience fulfillment today?

_____

_____

_____

_____

_____

_____

_____

_____

_____

What could I do in the future to experience more fulfillment?

_____

_____

_____

_____

_____

_____

_____

_____

_____

Morning

Date: _____

The three things I am most grateful for today are:

1.
_____
2.
_____
3.
_____

My top three priorities today are.

1.
_____
2.
_____
3.
_____

Today I will experience fulfillment through:

_____

_____

_____

_____

_____

Today I will serve others by:

_____

_____

_____

_____

_____

Evening

Date: _____

How did I experience fulfillment today?

_____

_____

_____

_____

_____

_____

_____

_____

_____

What could I do in the future to experience more fulfillment?

_____

_____

_____

_____

_____

_____

_____

_____

_____

Morning

Date: _____

The three things I am most grateful for today are:

1. _____
2. _____
3. _____

My top three priorities today are.

1. _____
2. _____
3. _____

Today I will experience fulfillment through:

_____

_____

_____

_____

_____

Today I will serve others by:

_____

_____

_____

_____

_____

Evening

Date: _____

How did I experience fulfillment today?

_____

_____

_____

_____

_____

_____

_____

_____

_____

What could I do in the future to experience more fulfillment?

_____

_____

_____

_____

_____

_____

_____

_____

_____

Morning

Date: _____

The three things I am most grateful for today are:

1. _____
2. _____
3. _____

My top three priorities today are.

1. _____
2. _____
3. _____

Today I will experience fulfillment through:

_____

_____

_____

_____

_____

Today I will serve others by:

_____

_____

_____

_____

_____

Evening

Date: _____

How did I experience fulfillment today?

_____

_____

_____

_____

_____

_____

_____

_____

_____

What could I do in the future to experience more fulfillment?

_____

_____

_____

_____

_____

_____

_____

_____

_____

Morning

Date: _____

The three things I am most grateful for today are:

1. _____
2. _____
3. _____

My top three priorities today are.

1. _____
2. _____
3. _____

Today I will experience fulfillment through:

_____

_____

_____

_____

_____

Today I will serve others by:

_____

_____

_____

_____

_____

Evening

Date: _____

How did I experience fulfillment today?

_____

_____

_____

_____

_____

_____

_____

_____

_____

What could I do in the future to experience more fulfillment?

_____

_____

_____

_____

_____

_____

_____

_____

_____

Morning

Date: _____

The three things I am most grateful for today are:

1. _____
2. _____
3. _____

My top three priorities today are.

1. _____
2. _____
3. _____

Today I will experience fulfillment through:

_____

_____

_____

_____

_____

Today I will serve others by:

_____

_____

_____

_____

_____

Evening

Date: _____

How did I experience fulfillment today?

_____

_____

_____

_____

_____

_____

_____

_____

_____

What could I do in the future to experience more fulfillment?

_____

_____

_____

_____

_____

_____

_____

_____

_____

Date: _____

The three things I am most grateful for today are:

1. _____
2. _____
3. _____

My top three priorities today are.

1. _____
2. _____
3. _____

Today I will experience fulfillment through:

_____

_____

_____

_____

_____

Today I will serve others by:

_____

_____

_____

_____

_____

Evening

Date: _____

How did I experience fulfillment today?

_____

_____

_____

_____

_____

_____

_____

_____

_____

What could I do in the future to experience more fulfillment?

_____

_____

_____

_____

_____

_____

_____

_____

_____

Morning

Date: _____

The three things I am most grateful for today are:

1. _____
2. _____
3. _____

My top three priorities today are.

1. _____
2. _____
3. _____

Today I will experience fulfillment through:

_____

_____

_____

_____

_____

Today I will serve others by:

_____

_____

_____

_____

_____

Evening

Date: _____

How did I experience fulfillment today?

_____

_____

_____

_____

_____

_____

_____

_____

What could I do in the future to experience more fulfillment?

_____

_____

_____

_____

_____

_____

_____

_____

_____

Morning

Date: _____

The three things I am most grateful for today are:

1. _____
2. _____
3. _____

My top three priorities today are.

1. _____
2. _____
3. _____

Today I will experience fulfillment through:

_____

_____

_____

_____

_____

Today I will serve others by:

_____

_____

_____

_____

_____

Evening

Date: _____

How did I experience fulfillment today?

_____

_____

_____

_____

_____

_____

_____

_____

_____

What could I do in the future to experience more fulfillment?

_____

_____

_____

_____

_____

_____

_____

_____

_____

Morning

Date: _____

The three things I am most grateful for today are:

1. _____

2. _____

3. _____

My top three priorities today are.

1. _____

2. _____

3. _____

Today I will experience fulfillment through:

_____

_____

_____

_____

_____

Today I will serve others by:

_____

_____

_____

_____

_____

Evening

Date: _____

How did I experience fulfillment today?

_____

_____

_____

_____

_____

_____

_____

_____

_____

What could I do in the future to experience more fulfillment?

_____

_____

_____

_____

_____

_____

_____

_____

_____

Morning

Date: _____

The three things I am most grateful for today are:

1. _____
2. _____
3. _____

My top three priorities today are.

1. _____
2. _____
3. _____

Today I will experience fulfillment through:

_____

_____

_____

_____

_____

Today I will serve others by:

_____

_____

_____

_____

_____

Date: _____

How did I experience fulfillment today?

_____

_____

_____

_____

_____

_____

_____

_____

_____

What could I do in the future to experience more fulfillment?

_____

_____

_____

_____

_____

_____

_____

_____

_____

Date: _____

The three things I am most grateful for today are:

1. _____
2. _____
3. _____

My top three priorities today are.

1. _____
2. _____
3. _____

Today I will experience fulfillment through:

_____

_____

_____

_____

_____

Today I will serve others by:

_____

_____

_____

_____

Evening

Date: _____

How did I experience fulfillment today?

_____

_____

_____

_____

_____

_____

_____

_____

_____

What could I do in the future to experience more fulfillment?

_____

_____

_____

_____

_____

_____

_____

_____

_____

Morning

Date: _____

The three things I am most grateful for today are:

1. _____

2. _____

3. _____

My top three priorities today are.

1. _____

2. _____

3. _____

Today I will experience fulfillment through:

_____

_____

_____

_____

_____

Today I will serve others by:

_____

_____

_____

_____

_____

Date: _____

How did I experience fulfillment today?

_____

_____

_____

_____

_____

_____

_____

_____

What could I do in the future to experience more fulfillment?

_____

_____

_____

_____

_____

_____

_____

_____

_____

Morning

Date: _____

The three things I am most grateful for today are:

1. _____
2. _____
3. _____

My top three priorities today are.

1. _____
2. _____
3. _____

Today I will experience fulfillment through:

_____

_____

_____

_____

_____

Today I will serve others by:

_____

_____

_____

_____

_____

Evening

Date: _____

How did I experience fulfillment today?

_____

_____

_____

_____

_____

_____

_____

_____

_____

What could I do in the future to experience more fulfillment?

_____

_____

_____

_____

_____

_____

_____

_____

_____

Morning

Date: _____

The three things I am most grateful for today are:

1. _____

2. _____

3. _____

My top three priorities today are.

1. _____

2. _____

3. _____

Today I will experience fulfillment through:

_____

_____

_____

_____

_____

Today I will serve others by:

_____

_____

_____

_____

_____

Evening

Date: _____

How did I experience fulfillment today?

_____

_____

_____

_____

_____

_____

_____

_____

_____

What could I do in the future to experience more fulfillment?

_____

_____

_____

_____

_____

_____

_____

_____

_____

Morning

Date: _____

The three things I am most grateful for today are:

1. _____
2. _____
3. _____

My top three priorities today are.

1. _____
2. _____
3. _____

Today I will experience fulfillment through:

_____

_____

_____

_____

_____

Today I will serve others by:

_____

_____

_____

_____

_____

Evening

Date: _____

How did I experience fulfillment today?

_____

_____

_____

_____

_____

_____

_____

_____

What could I do in the future to experience more fulfillment?

_____

_____

_____

_____

_____

_____

_____

_____

Morning

Date: _____

The three things I am most grateful for today are:

1. _____
2. _____
3. _____

My top three priorities today are.

1. _____
2. _____
3. _____

Today I will experience fulfillment through:

_____

_____

_____

_____

_____

Today I will serve others by:

_____

_____

_____

_____

_____

Evening

Date: _____

How did I experience fulfillment today?

_____

_____

_____

_____

_____

_____

_____

_____

_____

What could I do in the future to experience more fulfillment?

_____

_____

_____

_____

_____

_____

_____

_____

_____

Morning

Date: _____

The three things I am most grateful for today are:

1.
_____
2.
_____
3.
_____

My top three priorities today are.

1.
_____
2.
_____
3.
_____

Today I will experience fulfillment through:

_____

_____

_____

_____

_____

Today I will serve others by:

_____

_____

_____

_____

_____

Evening

Date: _____

How did I experience fulfillment today?

_____

_____

_____

_____

_____

_____

_____

_____

What could I do in the future to experience more fulfillment?

_____

_____

_____

_____

_____

_____

_____

_____

Morning

Date: _____

The three things I am most grateful for today are:

1. _____
2. _____
3. _____

My top three priorities today are.

1. _____
2. _____
3. _____

Today I will experience fulfillment through:

_____

_____

_____

_____

Today I will serve others by:

_____

_____

_____

_____

Evening

Date: _____

How did I experience fulfillment today?

_____

_____

_____

_____

_____

_____

_____

_____

_____

What could I do in the future to experience more fulfillment?

_____

_____

_____

_____

_____

_____

_____

_____

_____

Morning

Date: _____

The three things I am most grateful for today are:

1. _____

2. _____

3. _____

My top three priorities today are.

1. _____

2. _____

3. _____

Today I will experience fulfillment through:

_____

_____

_____

_____

_____

Today I will serve others by:

_____

_____

_____

_____

_____

Evening

Date: _____

How did I experience fulfillment today?

_____

_____

_____

_____

_____

_____

_____

_____

_____

What could I do in the future to experience more fulfillment?

_____

_____

_____

_____

_____

_____

_____

_____

_____

Morning

Date: _____

The three things I am most grateful for today are:

1. _____
2. _____
3. _____

My top three priorities today are.

1. _____
2. _____
3. _____

Today I will experience fulfillment through:

_____

_____

_____

_____

Today I will serve others by:

_____

_____

_____

_____

Evening

Date: _____

How did I experience fulfillment today?

_____

_____

_____

_____

_____

_____

_____

_____

_____

What could I do in the future to experience more fulfillment?

_____

_____

_____

_____

_____

_____

_____

_____

_____

Morning

Date: _____

The three things I am most grateful for today are:

1. _____

2. _____

3. _____

My top three priorities today are.

1. _____

2. _____

3. _____

Today I will experience fulfillment through:

_____

_____

_____

_____

_____

Today I will serve others by:

_____

_____

_____

_____

_____

Evening

Date: _____

How did I experience fulfillment today?

_____

_____

_____

_____

_____

_____

_____

_____

What could I do in the future to experience more fulfillment?

_____

_____

_____

_____

_____

_____

_____

_____

Morning

Date: _____

The three things I am most grateful for today are:

1. _____

2. _____

3. _____

My top three priorities today are.

1. _____

2. _____

3. _____

Today I will experience fulfillment through:

_____

_____

_____

_____

_____

Today I will serve others by:

_____

_____

_____

_____

_____

Evening

Date: _____

How did I experience fulfillment today?

_____

_____

_____

_____

_____

_____

_____

_____

_____

What could I do in the future to experience more fulfillment?

_____

_____

_____

_____

_____

_____

_____

_____

_____

Morning

Date: _____

The three things I am most grateful for today are:

1. _____
2. _____
3. _____

My top three priorities today are.

1. _____
2. _____
3. _____

Today I will experience fulfillment through:

_____

_____

_____

_____

_____

Today I will serve others by:

_____

_____

_____

_____

_____

Evening

Date: _____

How did I experience fulfillment today?

_____

_____

_____

_____

_____

_____

_____

_____

_____

What could I do in the future to experience more fulfillment?

_____

_____

_____

_____

_____

_____

_____

_____

_____

How I Am Fulfilled in my Faith

_____

_____

_____

_____

_____

_____

_____

_____

_____

_____

_____

_____

_____

_____

_____

_____

_____

_____

_____

_____

_____

How I Am Fulfilled in my Family

_____

_____

_____

_____

_____

_____

_____

_____

_____

_____

_____

_____

_____

_____

_____

_____

_____

_____

_____

_____

_____

How I Am Fulfilled in my Fitness

_____

_____

_____

_____

_____

_____

_____

_____

_____

_____

_____

_____

_____

_____

_____

_____

_____

_____

_____

_____

_____

_____

_____

How I Am Fulfilled in my Finance

_____

_____

_____

_____

_____

_____

_____

_____

_____

_____

_____

_____

_____

_____

_____

_____

_____

_____

_____

_____

_____

_____

How I Am Fulfilled in Fun

Notes

Morning

Date: _____

The three things I am most grateful for today are:

1. _____
2. _____
3. _____

My top three priorities today are.

1. _____
2. _____
3. _____

Today I will experience fulfillment through:

_____

_____

_____

_____

_____

Today I will serve others by:

_____

_____

_____

_____

_____

Evening

Date: _____

How did I experience fulfillment today?

_____

_____

_____

_____

_____

_____

_____

_____

What could I do in the future to experience more fulfillment?

_____

_____

_____

_____

_____

_____

_____

_____

Morning

Date: _____

The three things I am most grateful for today are:

1. _____
2. _____
3. _____

My top three priorities today are.

1. _____
2. _____
3. _____

Today I will experience fulfillment through:

_____

_____

_____

_____

_____

Today I will serve others by:

_____

_____

_____

_____

_____

Evening

Date: _____

How did I experience fulfillment today?

_____

_____

_____

_____

_____

_____

_____

_____

_____

What could I do in the future to experience more fulfillment?

_____

_____

_____

_____

_____

_____

_____

_____

_____

Morning

Date: _____

The three things I am most grateful for today are:

1.
_____
2.
_____
3.
_____

My top three priorities today are.

1.
_____
2.
_____
3.
_____

Today I will experience fulfillment through:

_____

_____

_____

_____

_____

Today I will serve others by:

_____

_____

_____

_____

_____

Evening

Date: _____

How did I experience fulfillment today?

_____

_____

_____

_____

_____

_____

_____

_____

_____

What could I do in the future to experience more fulfillment?

_____

_____

_____

_____

_____

_____

_____

_____

_____

Morning

Date: _____

The three things I am most grateful for today are:

1. _____

2. _____

3. _____

My top three priorities today are.

1. _____

2. _____

3. _____

Today I will experience fulfillment through:

_____

_____

_____

_____

_____

Today I will serve others by:

_____

_____

_____

_____

_____

Evening

Date: _____

How did I experience fulfillment today?

_____

_____

_____

_____

_____

_____

_____

_____

_____

What could I do in the future to experience more fulfillment?

_____

_____

_____

_____

_____

_____

_____

_____

_____

Morning

Date: _____

The three things I am most grateful for today are:

1. _____
2. _____
3. _____

My top three priorities today are.

1. _____
2. _____
3. _____

Today I will experience fulfillment through:

_____

_____

_____

_____

_____

Today I will serve others by:

_____

_____

_____

_____

_____

Evening

Date: _____

How did I experience fulfillment today?

_____

_____

_____

_____

_____

_____

_____

_____

_____

What could I do in the future to experience more fulfillment?

_____

_____

_____

_____

_____

_____

_____

_____

_____

Morning

Date: _____

The three things I am most grateful for today are:

1. _____
2. _____
3. _____

My top three priorities today are.

1. _____
2. _____
3. _____

Today I will experience fulfillment through:

_____
_____
_____
_____
_____

Today I will serve others by:

_____
_____
_____
_____
_____

Evening

Date: _____

How did I experience fulfillment today?

_____

_____

_____

_____

_____

_____

_____

_____

_____

What could I do in the future to experience more fulfillment?

_____

_____

_____

_____

_____

_____

_____

_____

_____

Date: _____

The three things I am most grateful for today are:

1. _____
2. _____
3. _____

My top three priorities today are.

1. _____
2. _____
3. _____

Today I will experience fulfillment through:

_____

_____

_____

_____

_____

Today I will serve others by:

_____

_____

_____

_____

_____

Date: _____

How did I experience fulfillment today?

_____

_____

_____

_____

_____

_____

_____

_____

_____

What could I do in the future to experience more fulfillment?

_____

_____

_____

_____

_____

_____

_____

_____

_____

Morning

Date: _____

The three things I am most grateful for today are:

1. _____
2. _____
3. _____

My top three priorities today are.

1. _____
2. _____
3. _____

Today I will experience fulfillment through:

_____

_____

_____

_____

_____

Today I will serve others by:

_____

_____

_____

_____

_____

Evening

Date: _____

How did I experience fulfillment today?

_____

_____

_____

_____

_____

_____

_____

_____

_____

What could I do in the future to experience more fulfillment?

_____

_____

_____

_____

_____

_____

_____

_____

_____

Morning

Date: _____

The three things I am most grateful for today are:

1.
_____
2.
_____
3.
_____

My top three priorities today are.

1.
_____
2.
_____
3.
_____

Today I will experience fulfillment through:

_____

_____

_____

_____

_____

Today I will serve others by:

_____

_____

_____

_____

_____

Evening

Date: _____

How did I experience fulfillment today?

_____

_____

_____

_____

_____

_____

_____

_____

_____

What could I do in the future to experience more fulfillment?

_____

_____

_____

_____

_____

_____

_____

_____

_____

Morning

Date: _____

The three things I am most grateful for today are:

1.
_____
2.
_____
3.
_____

My top three priorities today are.

1.
_____
2.
_____
3.
_____

Today I will experience fulfillment through:

_____

_____

_____

_____

_____

Today I will serve others by:

_____

_____

_____

_____

_____

Evening

Date: _____

How did I experience fulfillment today?

_____

_____

_____

_____

_____

_____

_____

_____

_____

What could I do in the future to experience more fulfillment?

_____

_____

_____

_____

_____

_____

_____

_____

_____

Morning

Date: _____

The three things I am most grateful for today are:

1. _____
2. _____
3. _____

My top three priorities today are.

1. _____
2. _____
3. _____

Today I will experience fulfillment through:

_____

_____

_____

_____

_____

Today I will serve others by:

_____

_____

_____

_____

_____

Date: _____

How did I experience fulfillment today?

_____

_____

_____

_____

_____

_____

_____

_____

What could I do in the future to experience more fulfillment?

_____

_____

_____

_____

_____

_____

_____

_____

_____

Date: _____

The three things I am most grateful for today are:

1. _____
2. _____
3. _____

My top three priorities today are.

1. _____
2. _____
3. _____

Today I will experience fulfillment through:

_____

_____

_____

_____

_____

Today I will serve others by:

_____

_____

_____

_____

_____

Evening

Date: _____

How did I experience fulfillment today?

_____

_____

_____

_____

_____

_____

_____

_____

_____

What could I do in the future to experience more fulfillment?

_____

_____

_____

_____

_____

_____

_____

_____

_____

Morning

Date: _____

The three things I am most grateful for today are:

1. _____
2. _____
3. _____

My top three priorities today are.

1. _____
2. _____
3. _____

Today I will experience fulfillment through:

_____

_____

_____

_____

_____

Today I will serve others by:

_____

_____

_____

_____

_____

Evening

Date: _____

How did I experience fulfillment today?

_____

_____

_____

_____

_____

_____

_____

_____

_____

What could I do in the future to experience more fulfillment?

_____

_____

_____

_____

_____

_____

_____

_____

Morning

Date: _____

The three things I am most grateful for today are:

1. _____
2. _____
3. _____

My top three priorities today are.

1. _____
2. _____
3. _____

Today I will experience fulfillment through:

_____

_____

_____

_____

_____

Today I will serve others by:

_____

_____

_____

_____

_____

Evening

Date: _____

How did I experience fulfillment today?

_____

_____

_____

_____

_____

_____

_____

_____

What could I do in the future to experience more fulfillment?

_____

_____

_____

_____

_____

_____

_____

_____

Morning

Date: _____

The three things I am most grateful for today are:

1. _____

2. _____

3. _____

My top three priorities today are.

1. _____

2. _____

3. _____

Today I will experience fulfillment through:

_____

_____

_____

_____

_____

Today I will serve others by:

_____

_____

_____

_____

_____

Evening

Date: _____

How did I experience fulfillment today?

_____

_____

_____

_____

_____

_____

_____

_____

_____

What could I do in the future to experience more fulfillment?

_____

_____

_____

_____

_____

_____

_____

_____

_____

Morning

Date: _____

The three things I am most grateful for today are:

1.
_____
2.
_____
3.
_____

My top three priorities today are.

1.
_____
2.
_____
3.
_____

Today I will experience fulfillment through:

_____

_____

_____

_____

Today I will serve others by:

_____

_____

_____

_____

Evening

Date: _____

How did I experience fulfillment today?

_____

_____

_____

_____

_____

_____

_____

_____

_____

What could I do in the future to experience more fulfillment?

_____

_____

_____

_____

_____

_____

_____

_____

_____

Morning

Date: _____

The three things I am most grateful for today are:

1. _____
2. _____
3. _____

My top three priorities today are.

1. _____
2. _____
3. _____

Today I will experience fulfillment through:

_____

_____

_____

_____

_____

Today I will serve others by:

_____

_____

_____

_____

_____

Evening

Date: _____

How did I experience fulfillment today?

_____

_____

_____

_____

_____

_____

_____

_____

_____

What could I do in the future to experience more fulfillment?

_____

_____

_____

_____

_____

_____

_____

_____

_____

Morning

Date: _____

The three things I am most grateful for today are:

1. _____
2. _____
3. _____

My top three priorities today are.

1. _____
2. _____
3. _____

Today I will experience fulfillment through:

_____

_____

_____

_____

_____

Today I will serve others by:

_____

_____

_____

_____

_____

Evening

Date: _____

How did I experience fulfillment today?

_____

_____

_____

_____

_____

_____

_____

_____

What could I do in the future to experience more fulfillment?

_____

_____

_____

_____

_____

_____

_____

_____

Morning

Date: _____

The three things I am most grateful for today are:

1. _____
2. _____
3. _____

My top three priorities today are.

1. _____
2. _____
3. _____

Today I will experience fulfillment through:

_____

_____

_____

_____

Today I will serve others by:

_____

_____

_____

_____

Evening

Date: _____

How did I experience fulfillment today?

_____

_____

_____

_____

_____

_____

_____

_____

_____

_____

What could I do in the future to experience more fulfillment?

_____

_____

_____

_____

_____

_____

_____

_____

_____

Morning

Date: _____

The three things I am most grateful for today are:

1.
_____
2.
_____
3.
_____

My top three priorities today are.

1.
_____
2.
_____
3.
_____

Today I will experience fulfillment through:

_____

_____

_____

_____

_____

Today I will serve others by:

_____

_____

_____

_____

_____

Evening

Date: _____

How did I experience fulfillment today?

_____

_____

_____

_____

_____

_____

_____

_____

_____

What could I do in the future to experience more fulfillment?

_____

_____

_____

_____

_____

_____

_____

_____

_____

Morning

Date: _____

The three things I am most grateful for today are:

1. _____
2. _____
3. _____

My top three priorities today are.

1. _____
2. _____
3. _____

Today I will experience fulfillment through:

_____

_____

_____

_____

_____

Today I will serve others by:

_____

_____

_____

_____

_____

Evening

Date: _____

How did I experience fulfillment today?

_____

_____

_____

_____

_____

_____

_____

_____

_____

What could I do in the future to experience more fulfillment?

_____

_____

_____

_____

_____

_____

_____

_____

_____

Morning

Date: _____

The three things I am most grateful for today are:

1. _____
2. _____
3. _____

My top three priorities today are.

1. _____
2. _____
3. _____

Today I will experience fulfillment through:

_____

_____

_____

_____

Today I will serve others by:

_____

_____

_____

_____

Evening

Date: _____

How did I experience fulfillment today?

_____

_____

_____

_____

_____

_____

_____

_____

_____

What could I do in the future to experience more fulfillment?

_____

_____

_____

_____

_____

_____

_____

_____

_____

Morning

Date: _____

The three things I am most grateful for today are:

1. _____

2. _____

3. _____

My top three priorities today are.

1. _____

2. _____

3. _____

Today I will experience fulfillment through:

_____

_____

_____

_____

_____

Today I will serve others by:

_____

_____

_____

_____

_____

Evening

Date: _____

How did I experience fulfillment today?

_____

_____

_____

_____

_____

_____

_____

_____

What could I do in the future to experience more fulfillment?

_____

_____

_____

_____

_____

_____

_____

_____

Morning

Date: _____

The three things I am most grateful for today are:

1. _____
2. _____
3. _____

My top three priorities today are.

1. _____
2. _____
3. _____

Today I will experience fulfillment through:

_____
_____
_____
_____
_____

Today I will serve others by:

_____
_____
_____
_____
_____

Evening

Date: _____

How did I experience fulfillment today?

_____

_____

_____

_____

_____

_____

_____

_____

_____

What could I do in the future to experience more fulfillment?

_____

_____

_____

_____

_____

_____

_____

_____

_____

Morning

Date: _____

The three things I am most grateful for today are:

1. _____

2. _____

3. _____

My top three priorities today are.

1. _____

2. _____

3. _____

Today I will experience fulfillment through:

_____

_____

_____

_____

_____

Today I will serve others by:

_____

_____

_____

_____

_____

Evening

Date: _____

How did I experience fulfillment today?

_____

_____

_____

_____

_____

_____

_____

_____

_____

What could I do in the future to experience more fulfillment?

_____

_____

_____

_____

_____

_____

_____

_____

_____

Morning

Date: _____

The three things I am most grateful for today are:

1.
_____
2.
_____
3.
_____

My top three priorities today are.

1.
_____
2.
_____
3.
_____

Today I will experience fulfillment through:

_____

_____

_____

_____

_____

Today I will serve others by:

_____

_____

_____

_____

_____

Evening

Date: _____

How did I experience fulfillment today?

_____

_____

_____

_____

_____

_____

_____

_____

What could I do in the future to experience more fulfillment?

_____

_____

_____

_____

_____

_____

_____

_____

_____

Morning

Date: _____

The three things I am most grateful for today are:

1. _____

2. _____

3. _____

My top three priorities today are.

1. _____

2. _____

3. _____

Today I will experience fulfillment through:

_____

_____

_____

_____

_____

Today I will serve others by:

_____

_____

_____

_____

_____

Evening

Date: _____

How did I experience fulfillment today?

_____

_____

_____

_____

_____

_____

_____

_____

_____

_____

What could I do in the future to experience more fulfillment?

_____

_____

_____

_____

_____

_____

_____

_____

_____

Morning

Date: _____

The three things I am most grateful for today are:

1. _____
2. _____
3. _____

My top three priorities today are.

1. _____
2. _____
3. _____

Today I will experience fulfillment through:

_____

_____

_____

_____

_____

Today I will serve others by:

_____

_____

_____

_____

Evening

Date: _____

How did I experience fulfillment today?

_____

_____

_____

_____

_____

_____

_____

_____

_____

What could I do in the future to experience more fulfillment?

_____

_____

_____

_____

_____

_____

_____

_____

_____

Morning

Date: _____

The three things I am most grateful for today are:

1. _____
2. _____
3. _____

My top three priorities today are.

1. _____
2. _____
3. _____

Today I will experience fulfillment through:

_____

_____

_____

_____

_____

Today I will serve others by:

_____

_____

_____

_____

_____

Evening

Date: _____

How did I experience fulfillment today?

_____

_____

_____

_____

_____

_____

_____

_____

_____

What could I do in the future to experience more fulfillment?

_____

_____

_____

_____

_____

_____

_____

_____

_____

Morning

Date: _____

The three things I am most grateful for today are:

1.
_____
2.
_____
3.
_____

My top three priorities today are.

1.
_____
2.
_____
3.
_____

Today I will experience fulfillment through:

_____

_____

_____

_____

_____

Today I will serve others by:

_____

_____

_____

_____

_____

Evening

Date: _____

How did I experience fulfillment today?

_____

_____

_____

_____

_____

_____

_____

_____

_____

What could I do in the future to experience more fulfillment?

_____

_____

_____

_____

_____

_____

_____

_____

_____

Morning

Date: _____

The three things I am most grateful for today are:

1. _____
2. _____
3. _____

My top three priorities today are.

1. _____
2. _____
3. _____

Today I will experience fulfillment through:

_____

_____

_____

_____

_____

Today I will serve others by:

_____

_____

_____

_____

_____

Evening

Date: _____

How did I experience fulfillment today?

_____

_____

_____

_____

_____

_____

_____

_____

What could I do in the future to experience more fulfillment?

_____

_____

_____

_____

_____

_____

_____

_____

Notes

Notes

Notes

Notes

Notes

Notes

Notes

Notes

Notes

Notes

Notes

Notes

Notes

Notes

Notes

Notes

Notes

Notes

Notes

Notes

Notes

Notes

Notes

Notes

Notes

Notes

Notes

Notes

Notes

Notes

Notes

Notes

Notes

Notes

Notes

Notes

Notes

Notes

Notes

Notes

Notes

Notes

Notes

Notes

Notes

Notes

Notes

Notes

Notes

Notes

Notes

Notes

Notes

Notes

Notes

Notes

Notes

Notes

Notes

Notes

Notes

Notes

Notes

Notes

Notes

Notes

Notes

Notes

Notes

Would you like to connect on a deeper level?

I invite you to reach out to me on my podcast or social media. Let me know how I can help you more fulfillment and increase your income while you're living in your purpose and passion.

Podcast
The Fuel Your Legacy Show

Instagram
@sam.knickerbocker
@thefuelyourlegacyshow

Facebook
@Samuel Knickerbocker

YouTube
Samuel Knickerbocker

Website
https://samknickerbocker.com

Also check out Samuel's other book

"Fuel Your Legacy: 9 Pillars to Build a Meaningful Legacy"